Plus

Tiger Sharks

WITHDRAWN

WITHDRAWN

by Deborah Nuzzolo

CAPSTONE PRESS
a capstone imprint

Pebble Plus is published by Capstone Press,
1710 Roe Crest Drive, North Mankato, Minnesota 56003
www.mycapstone.com

Library of Congress Cataloging-in-Publication Data
Names: Nuzzolo, Deborah, author.
Title: Tiger sharks / by Deborah Nuzzolo.
Description: North Mankato, Minnesota : Capstone Press, [2017] | Series:
Pebble plus. All about sharks | Audience: Ages 4–8. | Audience: K to grade 3. |
Includes bibliographical references and index.
Identifiers: LCCN 2016059068 | ISBN 9781515770008 (library binding) |
ISBN 9781515770060 (pbk.) | ISBN 9781515770121 (ebook (pdf))
Subjects: LCSH: Tiger shark—Juvenile literature. | CYAC: Sharks.
Classification: LCC QL638.95.C3 B357 2018 | DDC 597.3/4—dc23
LC record available at https://lccn.loc.gov/2016059068

Editorial Credits
Nikki Bruno Clapper, editor; Kayla Rossow, designer;
Kelly Garvin, media researcher; Gene Bentdahl, production specialist

Photo Credits
National Geographic Creative: Bill Curtsinger, 17, Jim Abernethy, 9, 15; Seapics/Andre Seale, 19;
Shutterstock: frantisekhojdysz, 1, 7, Greg Amptman, 5, kataleewan intarachote, 2, Luiz Felipe V.
Puntel, 13, Matt9122, 11, nicolasvoisin44, 21, Rich Carey, 24, Shane Gross, cover, Willyam Bradberry, 23

Artistic elements
Shutterstock: Apostrophe, HorenkO, Magenta10

Note to Parents and Teachers

The All About Sharks set supports national curriculum standards for science
related to the characteristics and behavior of animals. This book describes and
illustrates tiger sharks. The images support early readers in understanding the
text. The repetition of words and phrases helps early readers learn new words.
This book also introduces early readers to subject-specific vocabulary words,
which are defined in the Glossary section. Early readers may need assistance to
read some words and to use the Table of Contents, Glossary, Read More, Internet
Sites, Critical Thinking Questions, and Index sections of the book.

Printed in China.
004704

Table of Contents

A Taste for Everything

Night comes. A tiger shark swims up from deep water. Chomp! It catches the first fish it sees.

Tiger sharks live
in warm seas worldwide.
They eat more kinds of food
than any other shark.

6

Stripes and Spots

How did tiger sharks

get their name?

They have stripes like a tiger.

They also have spots.

A tiger shark has a wide snout and a long body. These sharks weigh about as much as a horse.

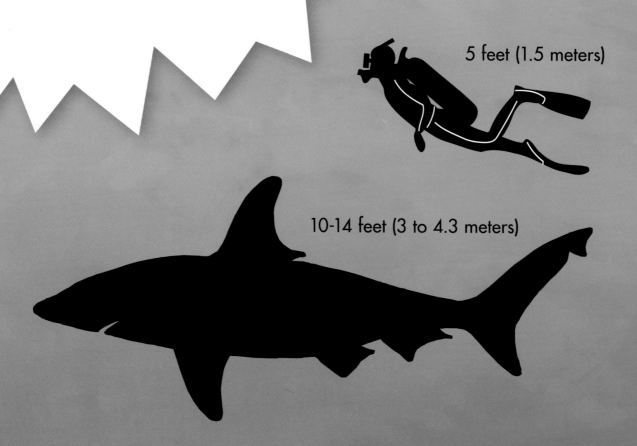

5 feet (1.5 meters)

10-14 feet (3 to 4.3 meters)

Tiger sharks have gills
on each side of their head.
Sharks use their gills
to breathe underwater.

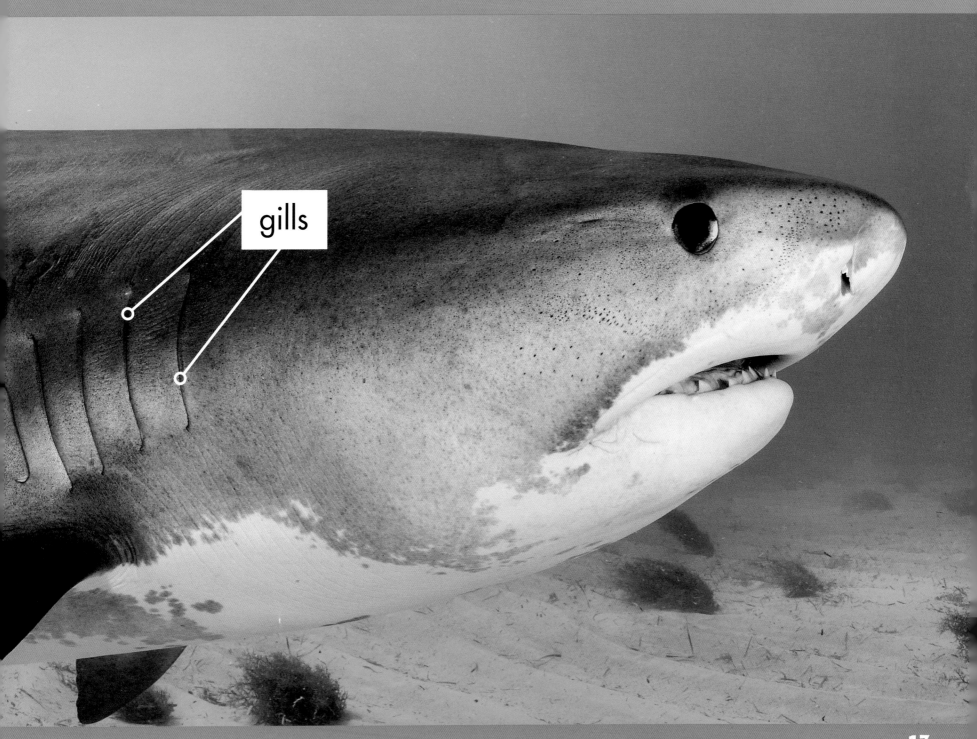

gills

Hunting and Eating

A tiger shark's teeth are sharp and jagged. Its jaws are very strong. Tiger sharks can cut open the shells of sea turtles and clams.

Tiger sharks eat almost anything. They hunt fish, sea snakes, and seabirds. Sometimes they eat trash such as cans and bottles.

Tiger Shark Babies

About 10 to 80 tiger shark pups are born at one time.

The pups live on their own.

They have dark spots and stripes.

A baby tiger shark's stripes fade as it grows. Some adults do not have any stripes. Tiger sharks live for up to 50 years.

Glossary

clam—a small ocean animal that lives inside a shell; clamshells are hard to open

fade—to become paler in color

gill—a body part on the side of a fish; fish use their gills to breathe

hunt—to find and catch animals for food

jagged—sharp and uneven

pup—a young shark

snout—the long front part of an animal's head; it includes the nose, mouth, and jaws

Read More

De la Bédoyère, Camilla. *Tiger Shark.* Discover Sharks. Irvine, Calif.: QEB, 2012.

Meister, Cari. *Sharks.* Life Under the Sea. Minneapolis: Jump!, 2014.

Waxman, Laura Hamilton. *Tiger Sharks.* Sharks. Mankato, Minn.: Amicus Ink, 2017.

Internet Sites

FactHound offers a safe, fun way to find Internet sites related to this book. All of the sites on FactHound have been researched by our staff.

Here's all you do:

Visit *www.facthound.com*

Type in this code: 9781515770008

 Super-cool stuff! Check out projects, games and lots more at **www.capstonekids.com**

23

Critical Thinking Questions

1. What are three things that tiger sharks eat?

2. What are gills? How does a shark use its gills?

3. How are a tiger shark's teeth different from human teeth? Why do you think they are different?

Index